TOURING BY BUS AND COACH

RICHARD WALTER

AMBERLEY

Front cover: Not specifically a tour but a bus service mainly for tourists. Stagecoach started up service 30 during 2023, running up the scenic Cairngorms Mountain from the centre of Aviemore. Named the Aviemore Adventurer, Plaxton Elite I Volvo B11RT 5421 (ST62 CZN) carries a unique and eye-catching vinyl branding.

Back cover: Garnetts Coaches, based in Bishop Aukland, offer five-star executive day trips, holidays, school contracts and private hire. Plaxton Panther Volvo B8R YX17 OJD is seen on tour in the centre of Blackpool.

First published 2024

Amberley Publishing
The Hill, Stroud
Gloucestershire, GL5 4EP

www.amberley-books.com

ISBN 978 1 3981 0706 9 (print)
ISBN 978 1 3981 0707 6 (ebook)

British Library Cataloguing in Publication Data.
A catalogue record for this book is available from the British Library.

Origination by Amberley Publishing.
Printed in the UK.

Contents

Introduction

The coach industry is indeed a fascinating one. Operations vary from family-run businesses of all sizes, big and small, to divisions of large bus companies or franchised units recognisable in the UK and even worldwide. Some come and go very quickly whilst others have survived and adapted quickly to changing demands.

Covid-19 and other global events have brought all sort of uncertainties to bus and coach operators across the world. Untold damage was done during the peak of the pandemic in 2020/21, with companies folding, reduced passenger usage, fewer orders for new vehicles, a reduction in financial assistance from the government after initial help in the lockdowns, high staff sickness rates and indeed difficulties with the supply of materials to bus and coach manufacturers. Escalating fuel costs was another underlying issue. Twice during 2020 – on 20 July and 1 September – hundreds of coach drivers honked their horns in central London for the Honk for Hope campaign in a bid to draw attention to the crisis facing the industry due to the coronavirus pandemic and looking for government support. A smaller procession of coaches took part in Edinburgh on 6 August 2020. A chapter in the book illustrates some of the participants, old and new, from small and large operators. I have included a significant number of photos from these days as they demonstrate just how varied and colourful coach companies can be in terms of age and variety of vehicles. Sadly, the loss of trade during the pandemic saw many familiar operators disappear forever or cut back on their services.

In addition to these challenging days, everything has been moving towards a desire to achieve early net zero, with fewer emissions and more 'clean' vehicles on the roads. Whilst service bus operators have been quick to start building up electric and hydrogen fleets, coach operators have been more hesitant, given the infrastructure problems associated with powering up coaches on long-distance work. Of course, coach manufacturers including Yutong have lost no time in developing options, with examples now appearing throughout the UK.

One of the more positive things to come out of Covid-19, however, was the increased demand for 'staycation' holidays; the rise in the number of bookings greatly aided surviving coach operators. Although foreign travel has since become popular once more, UK destinations and themed holidays still sell well. Whilst healthy bookings are a good thing, coach operators have also faced other problem factors. In many cities, towns and villages, places for coaches to park are now restricted and are very difficult to access. Passengers do not appreciate being set down and picked up far from where they are wanting to go. Likewise, drivers need to know the best options, and tour arrangers have to be aware of potential difficulties. Tour schedules can require short-notice changes, with alterative locations visited if some are not coach friendly. And if some journeys involve going on ferries, weather and availability of vessels can cause all sorts of difficulties in keeping to times and routes.

Meanwhile, open-top bus tours have regained their popularity. There are a huge variety available up and down the country, and overseas too, with some now in transition to being repowered or delivered as brand-new electric buses. In addition to illustrating some of those available in the UK, I've included a few recent photos from Dublin, which I hope are interesting and representative of the tours you can expect to see. Along with the traditional hop-on, hop-off-style tours, there are open- and closed-top buses offering murder mystery, ghost trips, afternoon tea, full meals, prosecco and even beer gardens. The iconic London Routemaster bus provides many of these tours, but equally there are more modern vehicles that also operate these fun events.

The photos in this book cover the last six years or so. With so many companies around I can only show a small proportion of them, and because I live in Scotland lots of the photos have been taken this side of the border. There is, however, a good selection of different manufacturers, bodywork styles and seating capacities. With such constant development and change, it will be interesting to see how things progress over the next few years.

My grateful thanks go to Andrew Chalmers, Scott Hutchison, Mark Lyons, Donald Macarthur, Steven Macaskill and Richard Sharman for providing some excellent photos. All are credited for their particular work. The uncredited pictures were taken by me.

Richard Walter, October 2024

Open-top electric buses could be a common sight soon. In summer 2024, West Coast Motors introduced ten new open-top Wrightbus StreetDeck BEV Electroliners to complement its diesel open-toppers on its red and yellow City Sightseeing Glasgow tours, with 12402 (SC24 WFA) being an example. The use of these buses align with Glasgow's strong green credentials and shows the operator's dedication to meeting Scotland's climate-change goals.

1
Coaches on Tour in the UK

Photographed in Blackpool on tour are Parks of Hamilton Volvo 9700s 290 WE and LSK 497 in Caledonian Travel branding.

Edinburgh Coach Lines Jonckheere JHV Volvo B11R PSU 616 is in Scottish Rugby livery but also operates tours and hires as it was being used in this photo taken turning onto Princes Street in Edinburgh.

Pictured in Fort William on hire to Lochs and Glens Holidays is AAA Coaches of Kirknewton Mercedes-Benz Tourismo DM18 AAA – new as demonstrator BU18 YRP to Evobus of Coventry.

Prentice of Westwood Coaches Plaxton Panther 3 Volvo B8R YX68 UCC in Harmony Coach Holidays livery turning into Glasgow's Buchanan bus station. (Andrew Chalmers)

Free The Coo Ltd (trading as The Hairy Coo) was established in 2010 by a couple of well-versed and enthusiastic Scottish tour guides who started with one bright-orange bus before fully investing in a business. Since then they have welcomed over 200,000 adventurers, expanding their tours, which cover all corners of the country. These two bright-orange MAN Neoplan Tourliners were delivered in 2024 with OU24 ZTE (*Laura*) heading the line-up for tours of the day.

The Hairy Coo fleet have a number of Yutong TC9s, such as SG73 TYV (named *Annie*) awaiting picking up passengers in Edinburgh on an early morning in April 2024.

Highland Experience Tours have a mix of large and small vehicles. One of their AOS Grand Toros (GU24 OKL) awaits passengers behind St Giles' Cathedral, Edinburgh.

Another Scottish operator is HAGGiS Adventures, who take their passengers by the horns and deliver them straight to the heart of Scotland's jaw-dropping landscapes. One of their vehicles is this Mercedes-Benz Unvi Voyager GT SN18 DZS (named *Baby Jamie* after its tour guide), seen in Fort William.

Timberbush Tours, one of Scotland's longest-running tour operators, celebrated twenty-five years in the business during 2023. Pictured at Lawnmarket is MAN Neoplan Tourliner OU24 ZTX.

Also at the Lawnmarkt departure point for Timberbush Tours is Unvi-bodied Mercedes-Benz Sprinter SL24 MGO.

One of a number of similar Volvo 9900s in the fleet of Lochs and Glens Holidays is SJ21 NDE, seen here passing through Abbeyhill in Edinburgh.

Earnside Coaches provide bus and coach hire in Perth, Kinross, Fife, Stirling and beyond. P20 BDR is a MAN Neoplan Tourliner and was photographed at the Broxden Park and Ride site, near Perth.

Cooper's Tourmaster Travel Ltd of Bedlington is a family business (established in 1953) that operate a wide variety of coach types. Plaxton Panther Volvo WSV 479 unloads passengers in Ullapool, with the ferry terminal visible in the background.

Mercedes-Benz Vario O816D Unvi PO62 CCE has been with a number of operators, but in this photo, taken in 2023, it was being operated by Radical Travel of Edinburgh in an attractive retro MacBrayne livery. It is seen on a tour leaving Edinburgh bus station.

Sky Coaches, based in Greater Manchester, have over fifty years of combined experience within the travel and entertainment business. Their Plaxton Profile Volvo B7R AT07 GYZ is seen here on a tour to Blackpool.

The distinctive Neoplan Starliner PO63 FMY of Howie's & Hearson Tours Designed (a family-run coach holiday company from Sheffield) parked outside the Discovery Point in Dundee. (Scott Hutchison)

The fleet of Pulham's Travel, Bourton-on-the-Water (which has served the Cotswolds community for 143 years), is always smartly turned out. Heading through Westminster in London is Plaxton Panther 3Volvo B8R BL19 PUL. In 2023 the bus and coach operator became part of Go-Ahead's Oxford Bus Company division. (Scott Hutchison)

Mercedes-Benz Atego Unvi Touring SN19 BKJ of St Andrew's Executive Travel passes through St Andrew Square in Edinburgh.

In March 2024 Lothian Motorcoaches (a division of Lothian Buses) acquired two Volvo 9700s including 9012 (SJ73 HVL), which is seen transporting cruise-liner passengers on a tour of Edinburgh on a rather wet morning.

Provider of luxury holiday experiences from its base in Henley-in-Arden, Warwickshire, Johnsons Coach Traveller's brightly liveried Irizar i8E Integral YP23 NCJ was pictured parked in Regent Road, Edinburgh, during the 2023 Edinburgh Festival. The operator is one of seven that were merged into The Coach Travel Group during 2024.

Rabbie's Trail Burners EVM Elegance Mercedes-Benz Sprinter 516CDi minicoach SL17 XFD passes through Pitlochry, a popular destination, on one of the many small group tours 'driven by curiosity and guided by storytellers'.

Another EVM Mercedes-Benz Sprinter in the Rabbie's fleet is SN23 TKK, arriving in Ullapool on its way to the Caledonian MacBrayne ferry for the crossing to Stornoway on the Western Isles.

Caledonian Travel of Glasgow is the UK's leading provider of short breaks and holidays by coach and has been in existence for over thirty years. Wearing the company's colours is Parks of Hamilton Plaxton Elite Volvo B9R LSK 508, also arriving at the Caledonian MacBrayne ferry terminal in Ullapool.

Caledonian Travel Temsa Safari HD13 AY23 DHD showing off its British Travel Awards 2022 logo on Princes Street, Edinburgh.

MR24 MPR, a Neoplan Tourliner of MPR Coaches in the livery of 'Globus family of brands' which includes Cosmos, on a tour through Edinburgh. Globus is one of the world's leading tour operators and its recognisable livery can be seen across the UK.

Aspect Executive Travel of Wishaw Bova Futura AGZ 1482 (formerly SN10 AUV) on hire to Tartan Travel at Halbeath Park and Ride in Fife. The company offers coach and minibus hire in central Scotland.

Doigs of Glasgow Mobipeople Explorer Scania K320IB4 YN70 YRD in the centre of Glasgow. Doigs is one of the largest coach companies in Glasgow, with a luxury fleet of over thirty vehicles.

McGill's Buses Mercedes-Benz Tourismo G0642 (90 JXY) dropping cruise-ship passengers from Greenock in Glasgow city centre.

In 2024 McGill's Buses set up Loch Lomond Travel, offering a variety of reasonably priced short breaks and holidays across the UK, from John O'Groats to the cliffs of Dover. One of the vehicles in the fleet is Yutong GT12 J0501 (SG73 TYX).

Shearings-liveried Higer Touring Scania N200 BRA of Manchester-based Bradshaws Coaches, who have over forty years of experience in coach travel. The vehicle is seen resting in Regent Road, Edinburgh. Shearings offer a broad range of fully escorted coach holidays to destinations across the UK and Europe.

Award-winning family company AT/Austin Travel of Earlston KNL 665, a Futura FHD2-131 VDL, carries 50th Anniversary 2016 logos looking very bright and shiny at Meadowbank in Edinburgh.

Simpson's of Rosehearty Mercedez-Benz Tourismo SM69 SUN on hire to Lochs and Glens Holidays in Buchanan bus station in Glasgow. The company was established in 1987 offering coach hire across Aberdeenshire. (Stuart Hutchison)

LA Travel Beulas Cygnas LA24 TRA, on private hire in Edinburgh, is one of the fleet of a family coach company established in 1997 serving central Scotland and beyond. It boasts a recently introduced new company livery of metallic grey and purple.

East Yorkshire Coaches Mercedes-Benz Tourismo 94 (80 EYC), seen in York, is part of a modern fleet of high-specification vehicles for all types of travel needs. The livery is very eye-catching.

Kineil Coaches, based in Fraserburgh, provide coach travel throughout the UK. Futura 2 VDL FN19 KCL is seen on the A835 between Ullapool and Inverness.

Wearing the branding of CIE International Tours (who operate tours throughout Europe) is Callinan Coaches Van Hool EX15M Volvo 231-G-3880 on a tour into Edinburgh. Callinan Coaches Ltd is one of the leading and most respected coach-hire companies in Ireland with a fleet of over eighty modern, luxurious coaches.

Also in CIE Tours colours is Edinburgh Coach Lines Higher Touring Scania K360IB4 YN22 YJM. The vehicle has subsequently passed to Ratho Coaches and been painted in their livery.

In Glasgow-based Tartan Travel livery is Marshall of Ashgill Setra S415GT-HD MHZ 9310 (new to National Holidays as NH13 CWH). It is seen here at Ullapool arriving for the Caledonian MacBrayne ferry to Stornoway.

London-based Goldline Executive Travel Irizar i4 Integral YN67 VDA near Edgware. The company specialise in leisure tours.

Resplendent in its purple livery is Hounslow-based Dhillon (Bharat) of London Yutong GT12 DN19 LON at Waterloo station. The company is one of the premier coach-hire companies in London.

Maynes Coaches of Buckie Royal Scotsman luxury touring train-liveried Neoplan Tourliner L24 GSM heading south from Inverness. Maynes has been around since 1947 and continues to expand and invest in new coaches for the fleet, actively exploring the scope for zero-emission travel.

An Ayr-based family business since 1910, Dodds of Troon operate Mercedes-Benz Tourismo V9 DOT, pictured with Edinburgh's iconic Deacon Brodie's Tavern in the background.

The Traveller's Choice Plaxton Panther Volvo B8R BV22 HBB in Glasgow. Founded in 1872 in the days of horses and carts, the company is based in Carnforth, Lancashire, and is one of the largest family-owned and -run coach operators in the North West. (Andrew Chalmers)

Eve Coaches of Dunbar, a family-run award-winning business that was established over forty years ago, was purchased by Lothian Buses in March 2024 to expand its own coach and tour offerings in East Lothian. Unique in the fleet is Optare Olympus Volvo B9TL Centurian E100 (0056 EVE) (previously Y10 EVE and new as SC09 ALL), which was Scotland's first tri-axle 100-seater double-deck bus when originally purchased.

Maynes Coaches of Buckie Mercedes-Benz Tourismo M17 YNE in a striking navy livery at Oban. (Andrew Chalmers)

Golden Tours of Alperton MCV eVoTor Volvo B11R 24 (LF19 FYD) in Bath. Established in 1984, Golden Tours are experts in tours of London, as will be seen later in the book. (Andrew Chalmers)

Available for a wide range of tourist, schools and private hire, as well as operating as a service bus on the Isle of Lewis, is Hebridean Transport Higer Scania HP72 HEB.

Skills of Nottingham Irizar i6s YS22 JGY in Edinburgh showing off its colourful and distinctive livery. With over 103 years of coaching experience, the Skills Group provide an award-winning choice of holidays through the UK and Europe.

Ratho Coaches added electric Yutong TCe12 SG73 TZA to its fleet in 2023 following the successful trial of a similar demonstrator. It was photographed on hotel shuttle work in the west end of Edinburgh.

A more traditional coach in the Ratho Coaches fleet is Scania Touring YT24 BUJ, seen in Edinburgh when new. It is used for a variety of hires, tours and special services.

There is no missing colourful Tamar Coaches of Plymouth Mercedes-Benz Tourismo TA18 MAR on a trip into Edinburgh. The team at Tamar Coaches have over thirty-five years' experience in coach transport.

A family firm since 1947, Docherty's Midland Coaches have an impressive fleet of executive coaches, including Volvo 9700 CS22 JDS, pictured in Inverness during 2023 on hire to the Scottish branch of the Omnibus Society.

In existence in Hertfordshire since 1946, Richmond Coaches' Van Hool TX11 Alicron 239 LYC whilst on an Edinburgh Christmas market run.

Showing off an eye-catching livery at Glasgow Cathedral is Rogerson Coach Travel Mercedes-Benz Tourismo DR23 RCT. Rogerson has over twenty-five years' experience and knowledge of coach hire.

Harry Ferguson Traveline of Bathgate in West Lothian operate Mercedes-Benz 1023L Unvi Voyager GT SN73 CYY, seen at South St David Street, Edinburgh.

Maynes Coaches of Buckie Mercedes-Benz Tourismo P33 GSM in John O'Groats Ferries livery in Kirkwall. (Andrew Chalmers)

Glenton Holidays provide national coach holidays direct from Scotland. Carrying the company's logo is Fife operator Bay Travel Coaches Limited Neoplan Tourliner OY23 CXO, parked outside the Caladh Inn, Stornoway.

Star Coaches of Batley VDL Bova Futura F2 VDL is spotted somewhat far from home at Waterloo, London.

2
Examples of What You Might See on a Tour

When Lothian Motorcoaches was established as part of the Lothian Buses family in 2018, a series of popular guided day tours were offered from Edinburgh. These next few photos show Plaxton Panther 3 Volvo B11RT 9001 (SN18 CVT) at various points on the Stirling tour, demonstrating the variety of attractions on offer in a day and showcasing why short as well as long tours remain popular in the UK. First stop for 9001 is Linlithgow beside the Cross Well, a spring well covered by a fountain shaped like an imperial crown which was erected in 1807. It is a replica of the original structure which was damaged by Cromwell's troops during the occupation of Linlithgow in the 1600s.

9001 pauses at the foot of the Kirk Gate, the entrance to Linlithgow Palace, birthplace of Mary, Queen of Scots, which is a very popular attraction for tourists.

The Kelpies are a pair of monumental steel horse heads between the Scottish towns of Falkirk and Grangemouth. 9001 arrives at the visitor centre car park.

Showing off *The Kelpies* to the rear of 9001.

9001 under the imposing Stirling Castle, which sits atop an intrusive crag which forms part of the Stirling Sill geological formation. It is one of the most historically and architecturally important castles in Scotland.

9001 taking a break from its tour in the centre of Stirling.

The magnificent Forth Bridges over the River Forth form the background for this photo of 9001. Connecting Fife and Edinburgh since 1809, 1964 and 2017, they consist of the Forth (Railway Bridge), the Forth Road Bridge and the Queensferry Crossing.

9001 in the grounds of Houston House, near Queensferry.

Posing beside the impressive Houston House outbuildings, 9001 shows off its striking bodywork by Plaxton.

Post-Covid, Lothian Motorcoaches ceased offering day tours but still offer private tour hires amongst other activities. Plaxton Leopard Interurban Volvo B8R 9201 (FSJ 674) (formerly Green Arrows SB19 GKE) was photographed in Pitlochry.

Stornoway's newly built Deep Water Terminal offers the largest cruise ships in the world a new gateway to the Outer Hebrides. Dwarfed beside one of the visiting cruise ships is Lochs Motor Transport ADL Enviro400 YX24 OVW, which gives an idea of the sheer size of the vessels. When the ships are docked, shuttle buses operate to and from the former bus station in the town's Church Street. (Steven Macaskill)

Lochs Motor Transport (which celebrated its seventy-fifth year of providing services on the island of Lewis in 2024) has four ADL Enviro400 double-deck buses as well as its coach fleet of modern vehicles to cope with the number of passengers arriving from the cruise ships. These are the first double-deckers to ever operate on the Western Isles. YX24 OVW is on its way to pick up passengers on a very sunny day. (Donald Macarthur)

A more traditional coach in the Lochs Motor Transport fleet is MCV eVoTor Volvo B11R SJ23 HSL.

Another shot of Lochs Motor Transport MCV eVoTor Volvo B11R SJ23 HSL, which is often used on a tour of the islands.

3

Tooting by Bus and Coach – Honk for Hope 2020

A hot sunny day in London in July 2020 and a campaign kicked off to raise awareness of the coach industry and how it needed support after the coronavirus pandemic had left the industry on the brink of collapse. Hundreds of drivers, bringing all types and sizes of coaches from operators throughout the UK, honked their horns as they drove through central London. North East Coachways from Peterlee, County Durham, Scania K360EB4/Irizar i6 *BIG Geordie* (M77 NEC, previously Y12 RLY) was one of the participants. (Scott Hutchison)

Johnson Bros Redfearn Travel-liveried Irizar i6 600 RT. (Scott Hutchison)

Johnson Bros VDL Futura 2 T3 JBT. (Scott Hutchison)

Murray & Son Executive-liveried Neoplan Starliner BM03 MAS. The vehicle was new as OU65 RLY. (Scott Hutchison)

Welsh's Tours of Pontefract sent Yutong G12 W10 HOL to the protest. (Scott Hutchison)

Mills (Yorkshire Rose Coaches) of Barnsley supplied Van Hool TX16 Acron D1 YRC, which had been entered in the 2018 UK Coach Rally held in Blackpool. (Scott Hutchison)

Unicorn Travel of Wrexham entered Higer Touring Scania K360IB4 RW19 UTW. (Scott Hutchison)

Reays Coaches of Wigton in Cumbria Van Hool TDX27 Astromega YJ19 BAO carries a very direct message in its destination screen. (Scott Hutchison)

The Honk for Hope movement arrived in Scotland on 6 August 2020 when around sixty coaches (many of which had taken place in the London events) gathered in Edinburgh. Maynes Coaches of Buckie Mercedes-Benz Tourismo N44 GSM is seen arriving at Sir Harry Lauder Road to join the parade into the centre of Edinburgh.

44 NN, a Jonkheere JHV2 Volvo B11R from the Penwortham-based fleet of Redline Coaches.

Parks of Hamilton sent Plaxton Panorama Volvo B11RLE demonstrator YX69 KZA.

Copeland's of Meir in Staffordshire Executive Bova Futura MIB 536.

Howard Snaith of Otterburn sent Plaxton Panther 2 Volvo B9R YN12 BBO in its very bright vinyls north of the border to participate.

Looking very smart in its corporate livery is Dodds of Troon Plaxton Panther Volvo B9R EE13 DOT.

Shiel Buses of Lochaber provide an abundance of touring work during the summer months, so sent Plaxton Panther Volvo B11R K77 SBL to participate in the parade.

Local Lothian operator AD's Taxis and Minibuses brought along VDL Futura X8 ACS to Honk for Hope.

David Ogden Travel of St Helens VDL Futura FHD2 integral YD19 GRU. The company offer holidays in the UK, Ireland and throughout Europe.

Murray & Son Neoplan Tourliner OU19 XXY. Sadly Murray & Son had gone into liquidation at the time of the Edinburgh Honk for Hope, but they still showed their support for the industry.

Tates Coaches of Luton Irizar i6 Integral YN64 LYF showing support in its windows.

Well-established family business Red Rose Travel of Oswaldtwistle Mercedes-Benz Tourismo UUI 7481 (previously BV10 ZKF).

Doig's of Glasgow 'Platinum by Doig's' Higer Touring Scania YT19 DZZ.

Another vehicle from Howard Snaith of Otterburn was Irizar HO17 WRD.

North East Coachways from Peterlee, County Durham, Scania K360EB4/Irizar i6 *BIG Geordie* (M77 NEC), previously Y12 RLY 3024.

Mills (Yorkshire Rose Coaches) of Barnsley supplied Van Hool TX16 Acron D1 YRC, which had been entered in the 2018 UK Coach Rally held in Blackpool.

Representing the smaller, but just as important, coach is St Andrew's Executive Travel Unvi Touring Mercedes-Benz Atego SN19 BKJ.

Andrew's of Tideswell tri-axle Plaxton Elite Volvo B12B(T) 476 BTO.

H&S Coaches Hire of Blantyre Neoplan Tourliner OU17 ORP.

Local Edinburgh-based and family-owned coach operator Festival Travel supplied Neoplan Tourliner *Isle of Arran* FSU 315 for the protest.

AAA Coaches of Kirknewton in West Lothian sent along Irizar i6 Integral AR19 AAA. The Travel Expert is one of the largest coach companies in Edinburgh.

Another local Edinburgh operator is Charlie Irons Coaches, represented by Unvi Mercedes-Benz Atego SN19 BHZ.

Walton's Coaches of Freckleton, Preston, showing off their Mercedes-Benz Tourismo BN17 JVA.

LA Travel of Kirknewton Mercedes-Benz Tourismo LA68 TRA in Eclipse Breaks livery, who offer a full range of holidays from Central Scotland.

Edinburgh Coach Lines Jonckheere Volvo B11R PSU 616 and Mercedes-Benz Tourismo SN16 DME in Silver Service livery arriving at the start of the procession.

Another example of a smaller coach was demonstrated by the appearance of Bay Travel Coaches Ltd Yutong TC9 P40 BAY. The company specialise in executive coach hire and bus services.

Anthony's Travel of Runcorn high-specification Barbi Galileo MAN RR2 RB16 ANT *Rosie*.

Charlotte Travel of Bonnyrigg Futura FHD2 VDL 66 CHT is one of a varied fleet of luxury and executive vehicles.

4
Rail Replacement

Ratho Coaches Yutong GT12 RA73 THO at Newcastle station performing a rail replacement service. (Andrew Chalmers)

Ross Travel Group of Featherstone Futura 2 VDL RT17 BUS also seen at Newcastle station on rail replacement duties. (Andrew Chalmers)

Bay Travel Plaxton Panther Volvo B9R L500 BAY (new to Lochs Motor Transport as YY14 NLK) on ScotRail work in Musselburgh, East Lothian.

York Pullman (now part of First York) Plaxton Leopard Volvo B11R R3 YPB picking up Northern Rail passengers at York station. (Andrew Chalmers)

Inverness-based D&E Coaches' Temsa MD9 Midicoach AM73 DEC in Edinburgh on standby for rail replacement work.

AAA Coaches are often called on to provide a number of rail replacement services in Glasgow. Parked near Central station is Mercedes-Tourismo JR72 AAA, which carries a message on the front in loving memory of founder James Renton 1956–2022.

5
Open-top Tours

A fine view over Scarborough with former Lothian Plaxton President Dennis Trident V523 ESC offering a Seafront Shuttle Service operated by Shoreline Suncruisers.

Tootbus (part of the RATP Group) have VLE 612 (LJ07 XEO) in their fleet on the Cardiff City Tour. It is an East Lancashire Visionaire Volvo B9TL, which originally operated as a partial open-top bus in London. (Andrew Chalmers)

Stagecoach South West frog-themed Alexander Dennis Trident ALX400 18307 (WA05 MGY) *Freddie* at Paignton, near Torquay, branded for the Golden Hop. (Andrew Chalmers)

Golden Tours MCV DD103 Volvo B9TL partial open-top bus 116 (BF63 HDJ) started its working life in London but now provides tours of York.

Go North East Plaxton President Volvo B7TL 6998 (794 EYD) undertaking the Toon Tour of Newcastle.

First Wessex, Dorset and South Somerset Sunseeker-liveried Plaxton President Volvo B7TL 32103 (MIG 4760) heading to St Ives from Penzance. (Andrew Chalmers)

Since 2014, RATP Dev has developed hop-on, hop-off open-top sightseeing services. The sightseeing team mainly operate in four subsidiaries spread over Paris, London, Bath, Bristol, Cardiff and Brussels under one common brand: Tootbus. Optare Visionaire Volvo B9TL VXE 728 (YJ11 TVM) is seen on the company's London Yellow Tour.

Tootbus Optare Visionaire Volvo B9TL VXE 730 (YJ11 TVO) at Westminster.

Tootbus YXY 791 (LS66 OLS) promoting that it is 'Planet Friendly'. Currently 60 per cent of the fleet is clean as buses are converted to reduce CO_2 emissions. The company is highly supportive of 'green' tourism solutions and launched the first 100 per cent sightseeing green fleet in Brussels in 2021, with other fleets being converted.

Tootbus VXE 792 (LS66 OLT) at Victoria with a vinyl wrap for Explore Taiwan.

The City Sightseeing-branded City Tour London by Julia Travel. Scania N230UD OmniCity 15025 (LX58 CFU) at Waterloo.

Fully loaded Julia Travel Scania N230UD OmniCity 15048 (LX09 ABO). The company operate a Red Route showing the key sights and top attractions of the city, whilst a Blue Route covers all prominent museums located in the heart of West London.

City Tour London by Julia Travel ADL Enviro400 19762 (LX11 BEJ) on the Green Route Shuttle, which offers connections to the Red Route.

Launched in New York City in 2016 and now operating in London in 2023, brightly branded TopView Sightseeing buses operate live guided tours of the city. Scania OmniCity 413 (YT59 RXS) was previously SP 69 in the Transdev London Sovereign fleet.

Big Bus Tours is the largest operator of open-top-bus sightseeing tours in the world, founded in May 2011. AN327 (LJ12 GKL) is an Anhui Ankai PO57/25D partial open-top bus at Trafalgar Square.

Golden Tours of Alperton offer, amongst other things, hop-on, hop-off tours of London. Most buses wear a blue and white livery but a few are decorated, like MCV EvoSeti Volvo B5TL 129 (BD16 YEG) which carries an all-over advertising wrap (including over windows) for Isabel Marant. One has to wonder how many perfect views of London passengers will experience on the lower deck through the contravision.

Similar Golden Tours MCV EvoSeti Volvo B5TL 125 (BD16 YEB) passes the side of St Pancras station.

Some of the Golden Tours fleet provides a hop-on, hop-off tour of Windsor, such as MCV EvoSeti Volvo B5TL 132 (BD16 YEL), photographed near Windsor Castle.

First Kernow Plaxton President Volvo B7TL 32209 (OIG 1795) performing the Land's End Coaster service at St Ives on Cornwall's spectacular coast. (Andrew Chalmers)

Also in Land's End Coaster livery is First Kernow Wright Eclipse Gemini Volvo B7TL 37058 (YJ06 XMK). (Andrew Chalmers)

Big Bus Tours Dublin Wrightbus Gemini 3 Volvo B5TL 181-KE-3872 in the centre of Dublin's fair city. Dublin has always had a choice of open-top bus operators, although some have now vanished. This bus when new was in City Sightseeing livery.

The 2022 St Patrick's Festival procession in Dublin was led by Dublin Bus Alexander Dennis Enviro400 Volvo B9TL partial open-topper EV49 (07-D-30049) in a special livery.

Dublin Bus offer their popular DoDublin hop-on, hop-off tours of the city. Alexander Dennis Volvo B7TL AX496 (06-D-30496) is an example of the vehicles used in the current livery.

City Sightseeing-branded Transdev York ADL Enviro400 4001 (S100 YRK, previously SN09 CEJ) picking up passengers from York station.

Reading Buses lent out Plaxton President Dennis Trident 520 and numbered it 399 (V524 ESC) in 2021 to Cardiff Buses for a special Cardiff to Penarth service. The bus was new to Lothian Buses. (Andrew Chalmers)

City Sightseeing Bournemouth-liveried Ayats Bravo Volvo B7L EU05 VBJ. Unlike many City Sightseeing tours, which are run under franchise to other operators, this one is run directly by the company themselves. (Andrew Chalmers)

First Wessex, Dorset and South Somerset Portland Coaster Alexander ALX400 Volvo B7TL 32031 (OIG 6947) was pictured at Weymouth seafront about to climb Portland Heights and then to Portland Bill for the lighthouse. (Andrew Chalmers)

City Sightseeing Cambridge-branded Stagecoach East Wright Eclipse Gemini 3 Volvo B5TL 13810 (BV18 YBC) at the University of Cambridge. The tour passes all the historic landmarks that make the city so unique.

Go South Coast Purback Breezer-liveried MCV eVoSeti Volvo B5TL 1711 (HF66 DSX) in Bournemouth hotly pursued by City Sightseeing former Lothian Buses Alexander ALX400 Dennis 2 Trident T502 SSG. (Andrew Chalmers)

During 2021 Shoreline Suncruisers of Scarborough bought two former Lothian open-topper Plaxton President Dennis Trident 2s, including V517 ESC, pictured at the Scarborough Spa turning circle. The bus, shown on service 109, has now been registered L444 SSB.

East Yorkshire Beachcomber vinyled Wright Eclipse Gemini Volvo B7TL 890 (BX55 XMC) is the ideal way to enjoy stunning upper-deck views of the sea and sand in Scarborough and the wider Yorkshire coastline.

An unidentified East Yorkshire Beachcomber-vinyled Wright Eclipse Gemini Volvo B7TL waits time before setting off on another Scarborough tour.

First Somerset Exmoor Coaster Scania N94UD OmniCity 36082 (SN57 DCE), which was new to Lothian Buses as their 994. The Exmoor Coaster is one of the most spectacular open-top bus rides combining the wild beauty of the Exmoor National Park and the seaside harbour of Lynmouth. (Andrew Chalmers)

First Somerset Exmoor Coaster Scania N94UD OmniCity 36081 (SN57 DBY) which was new to Lothian Buses as their 992. With the traditional seaside resort of Minehead at one end and the traditional fishing village of Lynmouth at the other end, the Exmoor Coaster links these seaside towns across the dramatic moorland, traversing the insanely steep Porlock Hill as it climbs between coast and moor. (Andrew Chalmers)

On a beautiful summer afternoon First Somerset Exmoor Coaster Scania N94UD OmniCity 36082 (SN57 DCE) leaves Lynmouth for Minehead. (Andrew Chalmers)

At the Lynmouth end of the route is First Somerset Exmoor Coaster Scania N94UD OmniCity 36081 (SN57 DBY). (Andrew Chalmers)

McGill's Buses commenced a Bright Bus tour of Stirling during the summer of 2024 using Alexander Dennis Enviro400 8926 (LK08 NVO).

McGill's Buses run subsidiary company Xplore Dundee Bright Bus Tours in Dundee. Alexander Dennis Enviro400 8927 (LK08 NVP) was caught in the centre of Dundee.

In Edinburgh McGill's Buses offer a City Tour and a Britannia Tour under their Bright Bus banner. One of their Edinburgh vehicles is Wrightbus Eclipse Gemini Volvo B9TL 2908 (CKZ 35), previously registered BF60 UUJ, seen entering the Queen's Park in the centre of Edinburgh.

McGill's Buses operate a Boat and Bridges Tour in conjunction with Forth Boat Tours offering a unique perspective of Edinburgh and the iconic Forth Bridges. Seen leaving Edinburgh is ADL Enviro400 MMC 8951 (SN66 WHB).

Lothian Buses Edinburgh Bus Tours operate three different tours of the Scottish capital. Wright Gemini 3 Volvo B5TL 231 (SJ16 CTO) is in City Sightseeing Edinburgh livery and was photographed at the Dynamic Earth science attraction at Holyrood. In November 2023, City Sightseeing Edinburgh was named 'Best Operator' at the City Sightseeing Worldwide Annual Conference in Hanoi, Vietnam.

Lothian Buses Edinburgh Bus Tours Wright Gemini 3 Volvo B5TL 233 (SJ16 CTV) is seen at Holyrood in the green livery of the Edinburgh Tour, which has a live guide. Eighteen open-top buses of the fleet of thirty are to be re-powered to battery-electric by Kleanbus in 2024.

Lothian Buses Edinburgh Bus Tours Wright Gemini 3 Volvo B5TL 248 (SJ16 ZZP) on Queen Street in Edinburgh in the blue Regal Tour livery, which replaced the Majestic Tour in 2024.

For a number of years Lothian Buses Edinburgh Bus Tours Wright Gemini 3 Volvo B5TL 249 (SJ66 LKO), seen passing the Palace of Holyroodhouse on the former Majestic Tour, featured a unique and very stunning Edinburgh-themed wrap. The bus was displayed at the Euro Bus Expo at the NEC in Birmingham in 2016 prior to entering service. It has subsequently been wrapped in new vinyls for the Regal Tour.

Lothian Buses Edinburgh Bus Tours Wright Gemini 3 Volvo B5TL 230 (SJ16 CTK) on the Cobbles' Tour, which ran for the 2022 summer season. Particularly aimed at families, this tour featured mascot Cobbles the dog and was a shorter and cheaper option than the other city tours.

For a number of years, up until 2023, Lothian Buses Edinburgh Bus Tours operated a combined bus and boat tour to the Three Bridges at the River Forth. Wright Gemini 3 Volvo B5TL 232 (SJ16 CTU) was one of two vehicles in this orange and yellow livery.

The future of open tours is electric. In its journey to transform its fleet of vehicles to zero emission in 2023, Oxford Bus Company took delivery of eight Wrightbus StreetDeck BEV Electroliners to supplement three existing retro-fitted electric open-top buses on the City Sightseeing Oxford tour, such as 191 (BJ73 WVX). (Richard Sharman)

Another shot of 191 well loaded in the centre of Oxford. The new fleet contains additional features for passengers, including glazed staircases and roof lights to improve customers' views of the dreaming spires. (Richard Sharman)

In summer 2024, West Coast Motors introduced ten open-top Wrightbus StreetDeck BEV Electroliners to its Red and Yellow City Sightseeing Glasgow tours. 12405 (SV24 WFD) was photographed at the OVO Hydro and Scottish Exhibition Centre on the Red tour.

12407 (SC24 WFF) is another example. The use of these buses aligns with Glasgow's strong green credentials and shows the operator's dedication to meeting Scotland's climate-change goals.

6
Special Tours

Edinburgh Bus Tours Dennis Trident Plaxton President open-topper 219 (XIL 1481, but new to Lothian as W632 PSX) was suitably vinyled and used for special staff family tours to meet Santa leading up to Christmas 2023.

Edinburgh Bus Tours open-topper Volvo Wright Eclipse Gemini 3 B5TL 250 (SJ66 LKP) was suitably decorated and loaned to St Margaret of Scotland Hospice for Christmas 2023.

Stagecoach started up service 30 during 2023 running up the scenic Cairngorms Mountain from the centre of Aviemore. Named the Aviemore Adventurer, Plaxton Elite I Volvo B11RT 5421 (ST62 CZN) carries this unique and eye-catching vinyl branding.

Stagecoach Van Hool Astromega 50309 (A2 XXW). One of two branded for a rather short-lived SuperBus.com afternoon tea tour of Edinburgh for the 2022 summer season.

Giving the phrase 'Let's Go Topless' an entirely new meaning, Roe Leyland Olympian ONLXB/1R C147 KBT was no stranger to Edinburgh when it returned during the 2023 Edinburgh Fringe to become an open-air venue for a comedy act. As part of a long history of different owners it spent time in the capital with open-top tour operator Guide Friday.

Another shot of C147 KBT, dwarfed by the mighty Edinburgh Castle.

Londoner Buses operate Heritage Route 15 between Trafalgar Square and Tower Hill using iconic London Routemaster buses. RM 1941 (ALD 941B) on the original tourist route A leaving Waterloo station.

Londoner Buses Routemaster RM 1357 (357 CLT) at Trafalgar Square.

For Christmas 2023, Londoner Buses operated suitably festively decorated silver Routemaster SRM 3 (650 DYE). (Mark Lyons)

The official Paddington Afternoon Tea Bus London Sightseeing Tour runs from Wednesdays to Sundays and, according to the blurb, is a 'pawfect' treat not to be missed. The tour, which comes with a special built-in screen providing a Paddington-guided animation, voiced by the famous bear himself and Mrs Bird, is operated by renowned operator Brigit's Bakery on genuine London Routemaster buses such as AEC RM1790 (790 DYE).

Premium Tours have a wide range of luxury coach tours and vintage open-top London bus tours. Park Royal AEC Routemaster RM1979 (ALD 979B) is seen operating the View from the Shard London Bus Experience with optional tea on offer.

London Retro Bus Hire of Longfield operate AEC Routemaster RML 2702 (SMF 702F) on wedding hires. The bus was new to London Transport at Upton Park bus garage. (Andrew Chalmers)

A somewhat more colourful tour full of craic and laughs is provided by Vintage Tea Trips in Dublin and Cork, who operate three fully restored and beautiful lovingly decorated AEC Routemasters such as *Pauline*, RM811 (ZV 10903).

The tours are often so busy that duplicates run, as seen in this photo of *Kitty* and *Pauline* in the busy centre of Dublin.

In addition to external vinyls the themed animal characters created for the tours feature on internal wallpaper. Try the warm, freshly baked scones made on board on this highly recommended tour which this author has sampled several times.

One of the other Routemasters operated on the Afternoon Tour is *Kitty*, RM2078 (ZV 11165).

Providing a local shuttle link with the Warner Bros Making of Harry Potter studio tour is Mullanys Coaches Alexander Dennis BYD Enviro400EV City EO32 (LG22 AYB), powered by Muggle electricity and leaving Watford Junction. The journey is no more than 15 minutes, so the fully vinyled windows should not cause major issues for passengers.

In London Bustronome operate state-of-the-art Ayats Bravo 1Rs, including LJ19 GNF. The vehicles have been converted into fine-dining restaurants, with a glass top allowing panoramic views of London and the stars. In this photo the bus is crossing a busy Waterloo.

Golden Tours operate The English Tea Bus tour in London. One of the vehicles used, shown here near Blackfriars, is former Metroline Alexander Dennis Enviro400 301 (LK07 AYZ). As well as offering a sumptuous afternoon tea, passengers can enjoy a glass of prosecco.

Passing by Waterloo is Golden Tours English Tea Tour Bus Alexander ALX400 Dennis Trident 154 (V154 MEV) formerly with Selkent. The brightly coloured vinyled buses are easy to spot on the streets of London. Note the fresh flowers in the upper front windows.

In 2014, Red Bus Bistro purchased their first Routemaster bus, which was quickly converted with a fully functional kitchen on board. A year later, in 2015, they began operating Afternoon Tea Bus Tours in Edinburgh, expanding into Glasgow in 2016. There are four Routemasters in the fleet with names bestowed on each. Seen in Waterloo Place in Edinburgh is Routemaster RML 2278 (CUV 278C), named *Nancy* after the owners' beloved mum.

Also in the Red Bus Bistro fleet is former Ribble Leyland Titan PD3/5 1847 (TCK 847) is named *Maisie* after their crazy second Labradoodle. As well as afternoon tours of Edinburgh and Glasgow where passengers can savour delicious homemade treats with tea, fizz or gin, the company also offer evening dining experiences.